by
Charis Mather

Minneapolis, Minnesota

Credits:

All images are courtesy of Shutterstock.com, unless otherwise specified. With thanks to Getty Images, Thinkstock Photo, and iStockphoto. Front Cover – Paper Street Design, ONYXprj, PremiumArt, Sergey Nivens. Images used on every page – Paper Street Design. 6–7 – Ghost of Kuji, CC BY 2.0 <https://creativecommons.org/licenses/by/2.0>, via Wikimedia Commons. 12–13 – ESO/L. Calçada/spaceengine.org, CC BY 4.0 <https://creativecommons.org/licenses/by/4.0>, via Wikimedia Commons, mapush. 14–15 – Jurik Peter, Sadoharu. 16–17 – Vadim Sadovski, Vladimir Arndt, Marusya Chaika. 18–19 – Vadim Sadovski, MR.Somchat Parkaythong, MASTER PHOTO 2017, Thomas Bethge. 20–21 – Antares_StarExplorer, Videohotdogs, ixpert, ESO/O. Furtak, CC BY 4.0 <https://creativecommons.org/licenses/by/4.0>, via Wikimedia Commons. 22–23 – Elena11, andrey_l, vchal, ktsdesign, 3000ad. 24–25 – Jurik Peter. 28–29 – L3erdnik, CC BY-SA 4.0 <https://creativecommons.org/licenses/by-sa/4.0>, via Wikimedia Commons, Cirone-Musi, Festival della Scienza, CC BY-SA 2.0 <https://creativecommons.org/licenses/by-sa/2.0>, via Wikimedia Commons, Grisha Bruev, Juri V, solarseven. 30 – Marina Sun, ImageFlow.

Bearport Publishing Company Product Development Team
President: Jen Jenson; Director of Product Development: Spencer Brinker; Managing Editor: Allison Juda; Associate Editor: Naomi Reich; Associate Editor: Tiana Tran; Senior Designer: Colin O'Dea; Associate Designer: Elena Klinkner; Associate Designer: Kayla Eggert; Product Development Specialist: Anita Stasson

Library of Congress Cataloging-in-Publication Data is available at www.loc.gov or upon request from the publisher.

ISBN: 979-8-88509-948-6 (hardcover)
ISBN: 979-8-88822-121-1 (paperback)
ISBN: 979-8-88822-268-3 (ebook)

For more information, write to Bearport Publishing, 5357 Penn Avenue South, Minneapolis, MN 55419.

CONTENTS

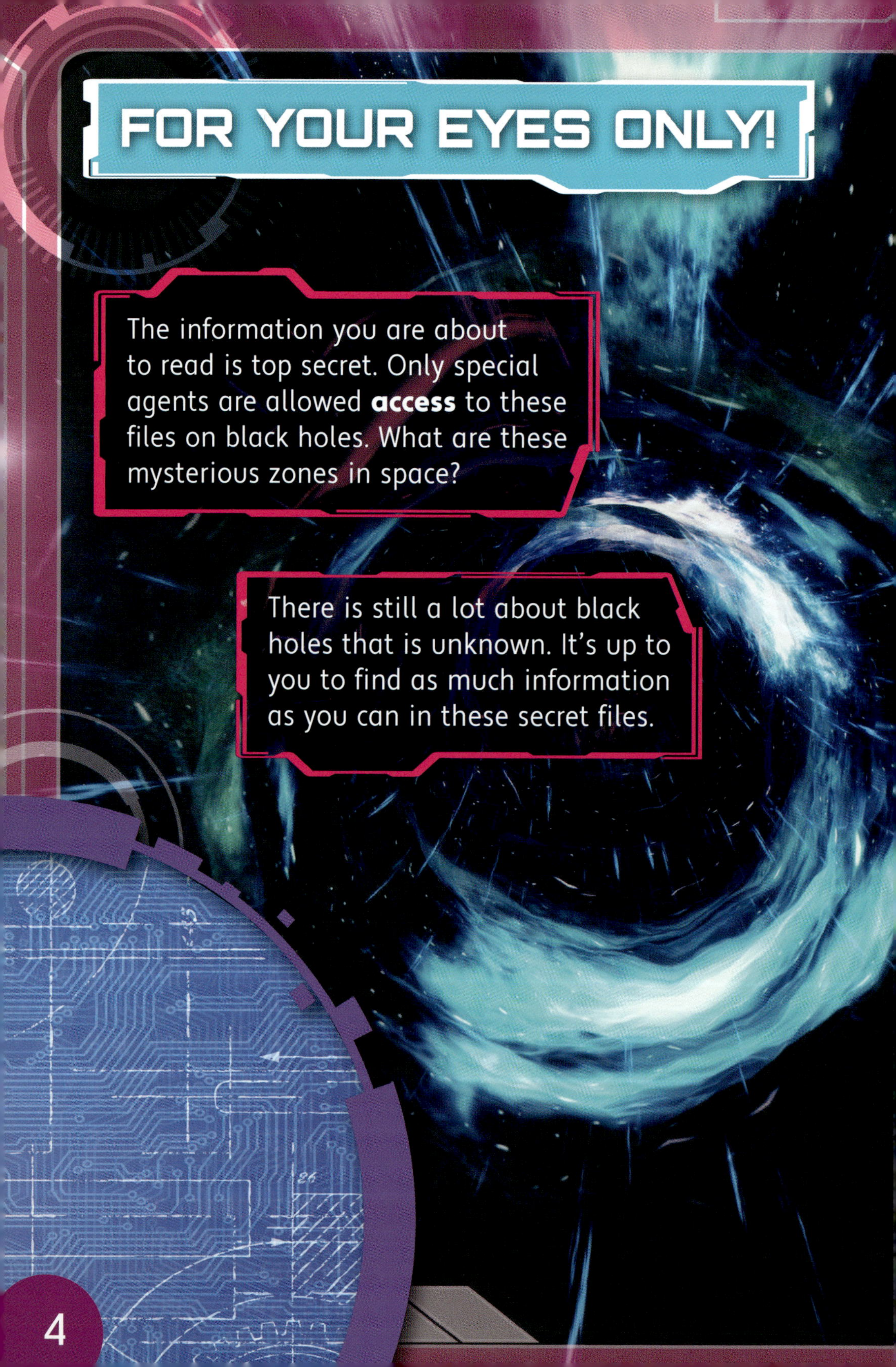

FOR YOUR EYES ONLY!

The information you are about to read is top secret. Only special agents are allowed **access** to these files on black holes. What are these mysterious zones in space?

There is still a lot about black holes that is unknown. It's up to you to find as much information as you can in these secret files.

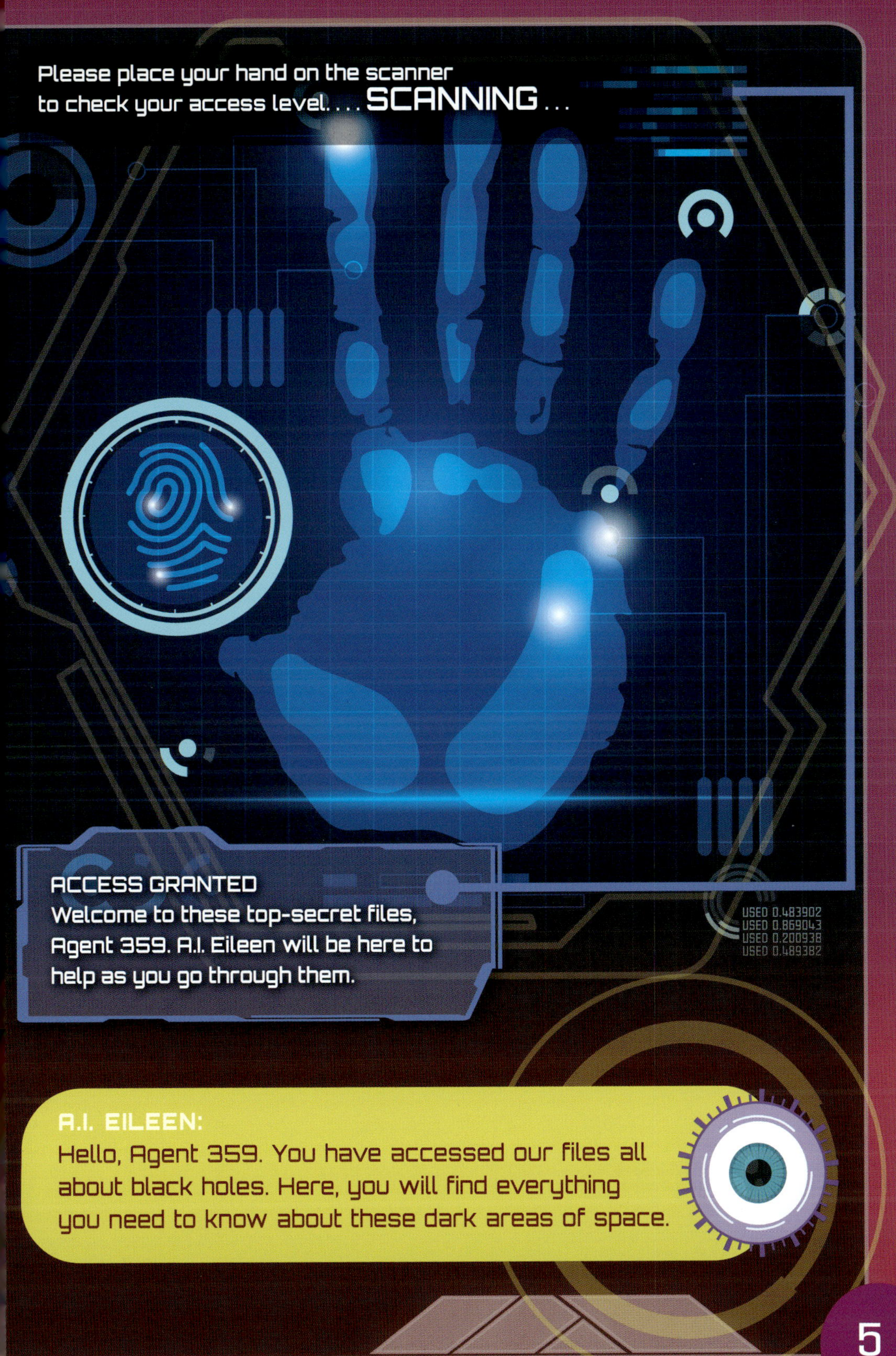

ACCESS GRANTED
Welcome to these top-secret files, Agent 359. A.I. Eileen will be here to help as you go through them.

A.I. EILEEN:
Hello, Agent 359. You have accessed our files all about black holes. Here, you will find everything you need to know about these dark areas of space.

BLACK HOLES BASICS

A.I. EILEEN:
Let's get started with some basic information about black holes.

To understand black holes, we first need to understand gravity. Gravity is the invisible **force** that pulls objects toward one another. Earth's gravity keeps you on the ground. It also keeps the moon in **orbit** around Earth and Earth circling around the sun.

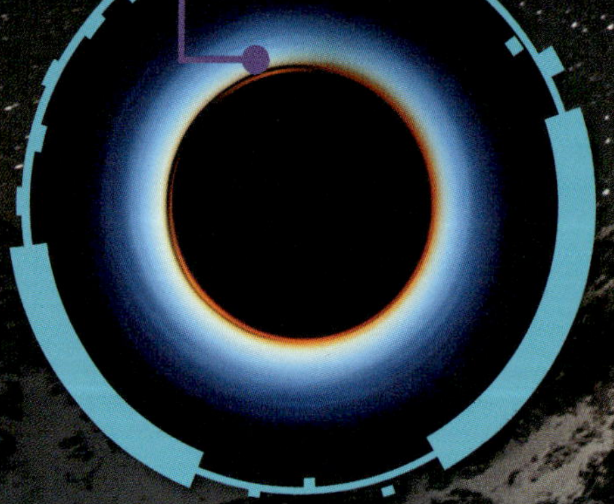

A black hole has gravity so strong that almost nothing can escape it–including light! Dust, planets, and even stars that get too close are sucked into the black hole.

The boundary after which light and objects cannot escape a black hole is called the event horizon.

The strength of an object's gravitational pull has to do with its **mass**. This is a measure of the amount of matter, or stuff, something is made of. Black holes have a lot of matter, often packed into a comparatively small space. Scientists usually describe the size of black holes by talking about their mass instead of how far across they are.

Lots of mass can be pressed into a small space.

A.I. EILEEN:
As a black hole pulls in matter over time, it becomes more massive.

TYPES OF BLACK HOLES

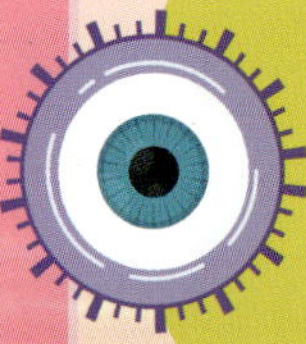

A.I. EILEEN:
Most scientists divide black holes into two main types: stellar and supermassive. Stellar black holes are relatively small compared to supermassive ones. Some scientists are also searching for medium-sized, or intermediate, black holes.

The city of Paris, France, is about the same size as some stellar black holes.

STELLAR BLACK HOLES

Scientists believe a stellar black hole is formed when a dying star **collapses** in on itself. Stellar black holes are usually 10 to 24 times more massive than our sun but are packed into a space just a few miles wide.

SUPERMASSIVE BLACK HOLES

Supermassive black holes make stellar black holes look tiny. The mass of a supermassive black hole can be billions of times greater than the sun's. While some of these black holes are the size of our sun, others can be as large as our entire solar system!

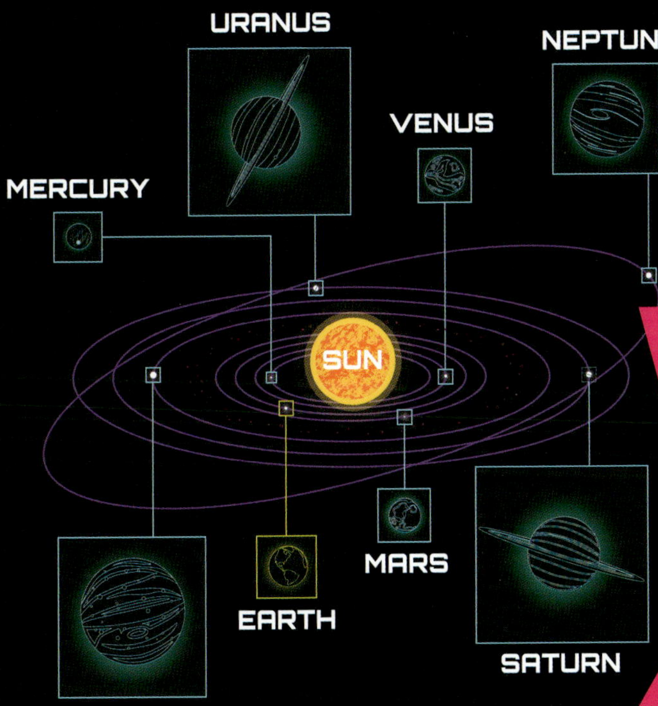

OUR SOLAR SYSTEM

Our solar system consists of the eight planets and all the other space objects orbiting the sun.

GALAXY NGC 4414

Most supermassive black holes have been found at the center of **galaxies**.

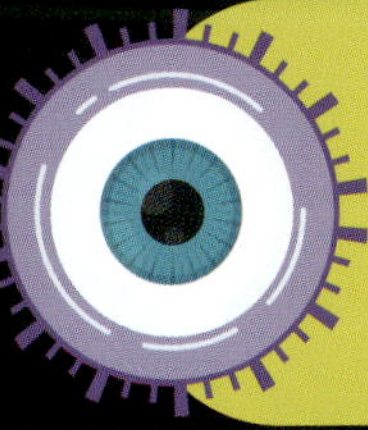

A.I. EILEEN:

Supermassive black holes can form when groups of nearby stars collapse or when smaller black holes join together.

DISCOVERING BLACK HOLES

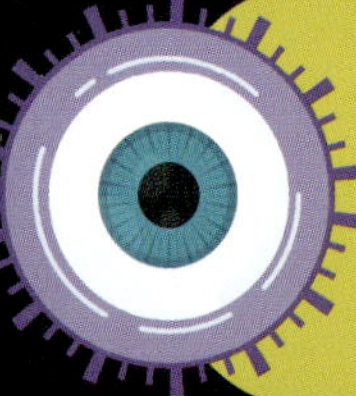

A.I. EILEEN:
Even before the first black hole was found, some people realized they must be out there. These scientists would have made great secret agents!

ALBERT EINSTEIN

Albert Einstein used math to study gravity. In 1915, he wrote that even light might be pulled into areas of very strong gravity and not be able to escape. Since then, scientists have proved that his ideas were correct!

KARL SCHWARZSCHILD

At first, Einstein thought his results seemed too strange to be true. However, a man named Karl Schwarzschild helped fill in the missing pieces of Einstein's **theory**. He also used math to explain how black holes could exist.

A.I. EILEEN:
Einstein and Schwarzschild's ideas **predicted** that black holes could exist. Today, scientists searching outer space have found them!

CAN YOU SEE A BLACK HOLE?

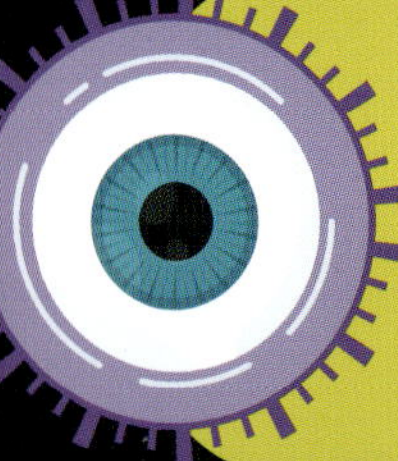

A.I. EILEEN:

The gravity of black holes pulls in all the light around them. This means they cannot be seen with a normal **telescope** or camera. Scientists use special **equipment** to **detect** black holes.

STARLIGHT BENT BY A BLACK HOLE

STARLIGHT NOT BENT BY A BLACK HOLE

LIGHT BENDING

Light normally travels in a straight line. However, if light passes near a black hole but not close enough to be pulled in, that light can be bent instead. So, although scientists can't see black holes, they can find black holes by looking for light from distant stars bending around them.

X-RAYS

Another way that black holes can be found is with equipment that detects **X-rays**. Some black holes have a lot of this invisible energy around them. The X-rays come from the intense heat created when matter is pulled into a black hole.

The Chandra X-ray Observatory is a space telescope that detects X-rays.

SAGITTARIUS A*

A.I. EILEEN:
The Chandra Observatory detects X-rays from black holes Sagittarius A* in the center of our Milky Way galaxy and M87 in the distant Messier 87 galaxy.

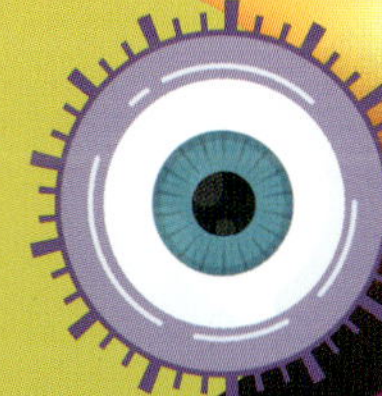

AN IMPOSSIBLE PICTURE

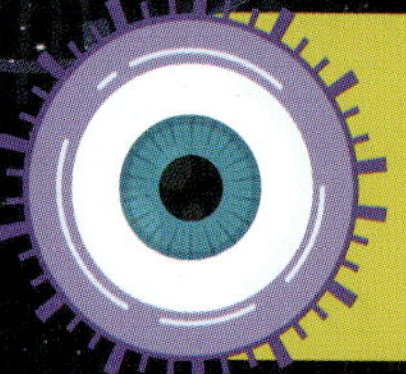

A.I. EILEEN:
Scientists also have special equipment that can take photographs of black holes.

Trying to take a photo of a black hole is like trying to take a photo of a black dot on a black piece of paper from a hundred miles away!

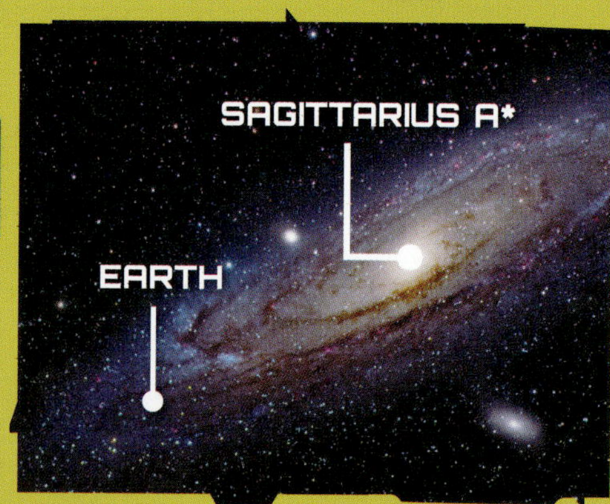

To take a photo of a black hole with a normal camera, you would need a lens as wide as Earth itself. Obviously, this is impossible. So, scientists decided to try using many smaller ones.

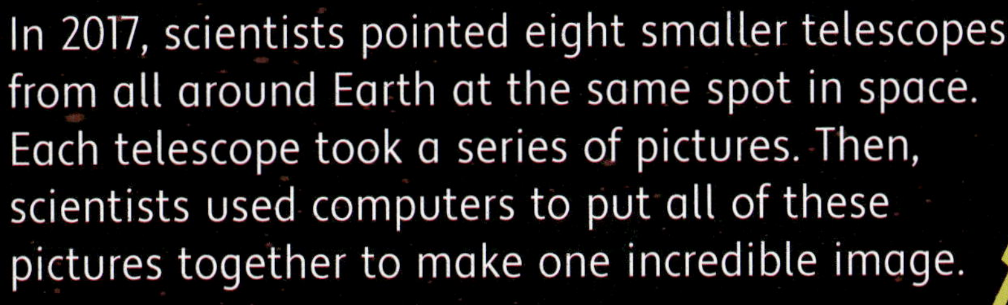

In 2017, scientists pointed eight smaller telescopes from all around Earth at the same spot in space. Each telescope took a series of pictures. Then, scientists used computers to put all of these pictures together to make one incredible image.

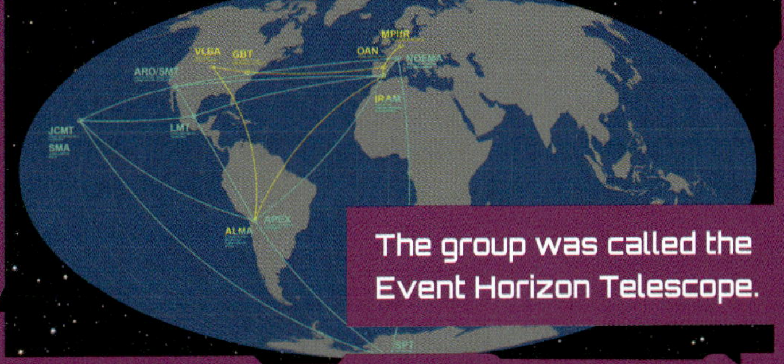

The group was called the Event Horizon Telescope.

This is the first picture of a black hole ever taken. It is a supermassive black hole at the center of the Messier 87 galaxy.

A.I. EILEEN:
In 2022, scientists took the first photo of Sagittarius A*, the black hole at the center of our own galaxy.

BLAZARS AND QUASARS

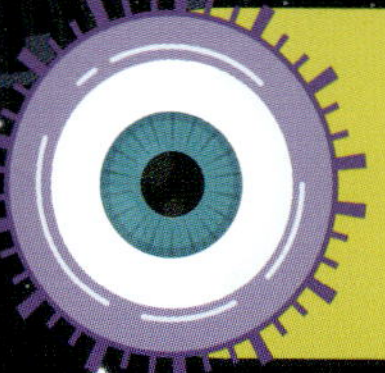

A.I. EILEEN:
Some of a black hole's matter can escape in the form of intense bursts of energy.

Supermassive black holes may have flows of **gas** and dust swirling just outside their event horizons. These are known as accretion disks. Some of this matter gets pulled into the black hole. But some of it heats up and then shoots away into space. When this energy burst is pointed toward Earth, it's called a blazar. When the burst is pointed in another direction, it is known as a quasar.

Blazars and quasars give out so much energy that they are called the brightest things in the known universe. Quasars can sometimes be spotted using telescopes, but blazars cannot be seen by our eyes. Fortunately, there is equipment that can detect them.

THE BLAZAR MARKARIAN 421

Although blazars are extremely powerful, Earth is far enough away to be safe from harm. One of the closest to Earth is still millions of **light-years** away.

DANGER ON THE EVENT HORIZON

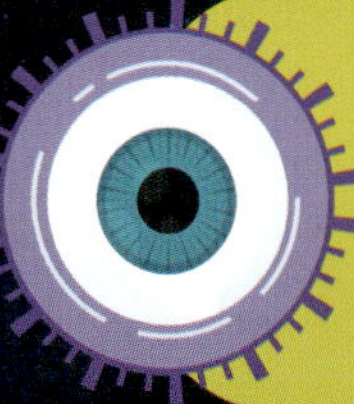

A.I. EILEEN:
Earth's safety is of top importance to our secret agents. These reports will tell you how dangerous scientists think black holes might be to our planet.

WILL EARTH BE PULLED INTO SAGITTARIUS A*?
Although the gravity of black holes is extremely powerful, the closest ones are far enough away that they can't swallow Earth. Even Sagittarius A*, the supermassive black hole at the center of our Milky Way galaxy, is more than 26,000 light-years away.

CONCLUSION
Earth is not in danger from Sagittarius A*.

COULD THE SUN BECOME A BLACK HOLE?

If a star is massive enough, it can turn into a black hole when it dies. Luckily, our sun doesn't have enough mass for this to happen.

Instead of collapsing into a black hole, scientists believe that when our sun dies it will shrink to become a smaller type of star called a white dwarf. This process would probably take around 5 billion years.

CONCLUSION
The sun will not become a black hole.

AVERAGE STAR

WHITE DWARF STAR

SPAGHETTIFICATION

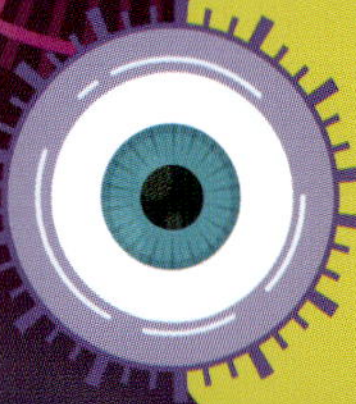

A.I. EILEEN:
Every black hole that we know of is too far away to be a threat to Earth. Still, that hasn't stopped our agents from figuring out what would happen if a human ever got too close to one.

If a human could somehow survive the energy and heat shooting out of a black hole, they would still have to deal with its powerful gravity. Gravity gets stronger and stronger as you approach the center of a black hole. Anybody approaching would be stretched by the pulling force.

If someone entered a black hole feetfirst, the pull of gravity would begin by stretching out their toes. Then, it would stretch out their feet, their legs, and so on up the body. They would become thinner and longer, just like a rubber band.

A person would not survive spaghettification.

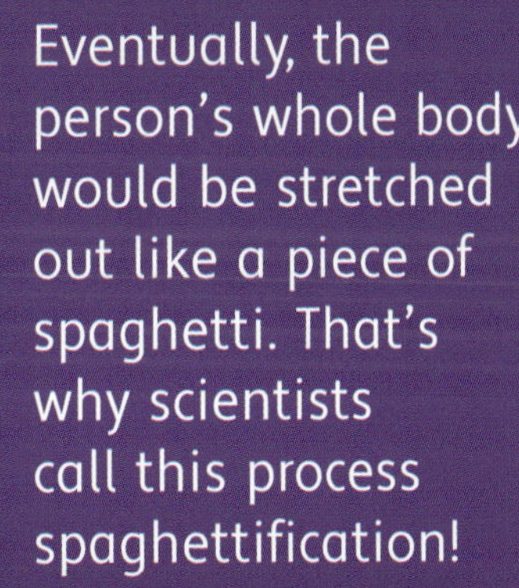

Eventually, the person's whole body would be stretched out like a piece of spaghetti. That's why scientists call this process spaghettification!

WORMHOLES

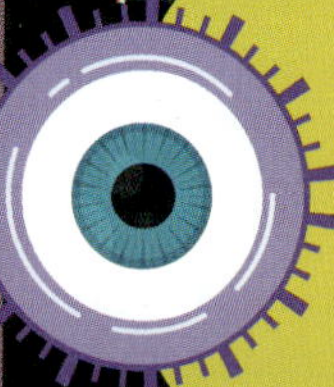

A.I. EILEEN:
In addition to predicting black holes, Albert Einstein wrote of a kind of black hole that has both an entrance and an exit! This is called a wormhole. To date, none of our agents has discovered an actual wormhole.

Black holes pull things in and trap them forever. There is no exit. A wormhole would be like a black hole that pulls things in but then spits them out somewhere else.

Einstein and a man called Nathan Rosen thought that if a wormhole existed, it might connect two distant areas of space like a tunnel or a bridge. For this reason, wormholes are also known as Einstein-Rosen bridges.

Some people think if wormholes are real, it will be possible to use them to travel to different galaxies.

BLACK HOLE CRASH

Two supermassive black holes known as PKS 2131-021 are circling around each other about 9 million light-years away from Earth. They are getting closer and closer to each other. At their current speeds, scientists believe they will smash into each other in about 10,000 years.

Each of these black holes is hundreds of millions times more massive than the sun.

When two black holes orbit closely around each other, they are called a binary black hole. After they crash together, they will become one larger black hole. This process is known as merging.

The merging of black holes causes waves of gravity to spread out, stretching and squashing parts of space.

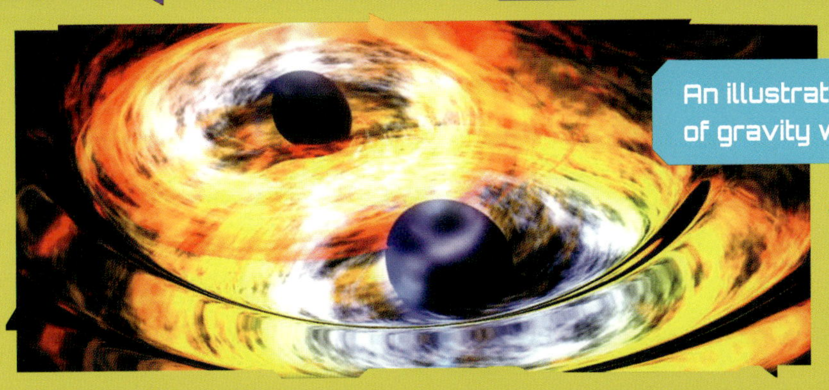

An illustration of gravity waves

Scientists can use equipment to detect the waves from merging black holes in order to learn more about the location of the black holes themselves. Fortunately, we haven't learned of any black holes close enough to Earth that these waves would be felt on our planet.

Equipment at the LIGO observatory detects gravity waves.

CYGNUS X-1

Cygnus X-1 is a stellar black hole more than 6,000 light-years from Earth. It is so close to a huge blue star called HDE 226868 that it is sucking in the star's gas.

CYGNUS X-1

Cygnus X-1 was detected in 1964, but it took 25 years for scientists to agree that it really was a black hole. It is one of the largest stellar black holes ever found, as well as one of the fastest-spinning. It rotates at a speed of about 800 times a second!
Cygnus X-1 can be seen with X-ray equipment.
HDE 226868
Cygnus X-1 is close to the star HDE 226868.

PENROSE ENERGY

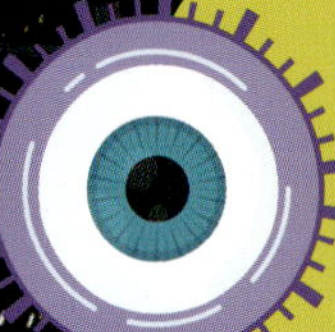

A.I. EILEEN:
Humans are always on the lookout for better energy sources. Some people think that in the future, we will be able to collect and use the energy created by black holes.

SIR ROGER PENROSE

Scientist Sir Roger Penrose thought black holes could be powerful enough to split tiny objects in half. After an object splits, one half would be pulled past the event horizon into the black hole. The other half would get shot outward beyond the pull of the black hole.

Tiny objects going around a black hole may split into two parts.

The black hole sucks this part in.

Energy pushes this part out.

Black holes spin extremely fast. Penrose figured out that this spin could push half of the split object away from the event horizon. Just like a wet tennis ball spinning through the air sends drops of water flying, black holes can use their spinning energy to send objects away from them.

A.I. EILEEN:
If humans are able to get close enough to black holes, they might be able to capture the energy that is **propelling** these flying objects.

YOUR MISSION

It's time for you to decide what to do with this top-secret information. Some of our agents continue to study math to learn more about space. **Astrophysicists** have made many exciting discoveries about space.

Your next mission is to pass on everything you have learned to a new, trusted secret agent. We need as many agents learning about space as possible. There's a lot more to find out! Good luck, Agent 359.

GLOSSARY

access the permission to go somewhere or use something

astrophysicists scientists who study space and the movement of space objects

collapses breaks apart and falls in on itself

detect to find or locate

equipment tools that can be used for certain jobs

force a pushing or pulling power

galaxies groups of millions or billions of stars and other space objects

gas airy matter that spreads out to fill a space

light-years the distances light can travel measured in relation to years

mass the amount of matter, or stuff, things are made of

orbit to travel in a circular path around something

predicted guessed that something would happen or exist before knowing for certain

propelling pushing or driving forward

telescope a tool for looking closely at things that are far away

theory an idea or guess that will be proved right or wrong by using science

X-rays waves of strong energy that cannot be seen with the human eye

INDEX

READ MORE

Finan, Catherine C. *Stars and Galaxies (X-treme Facts: Space).* Minneapolis: Bearport Publishing Company, 2022.

Goldstein, Margaret J. *Mysteries of Black Holes (Space Mysteries).* Minneapolis: Lerner Publications, 2021.

Labrecque, Ellen. *Mysteries of Black Holes and Dark Matter (Solving Space Mysteries).* North Mankato, MN: Capstone Press, 2021.

LEARN MORE ONLINE

1. Go to **www.factsurfer.com** or scan the QR code below.
2. Enter **"Black Hole Space Files"** into the search box.
3. Click on the cover of this book to see a list of websites.